Betty Crosson "Cade Lake" 1985
Box 824
Caldwell, Texas
77836

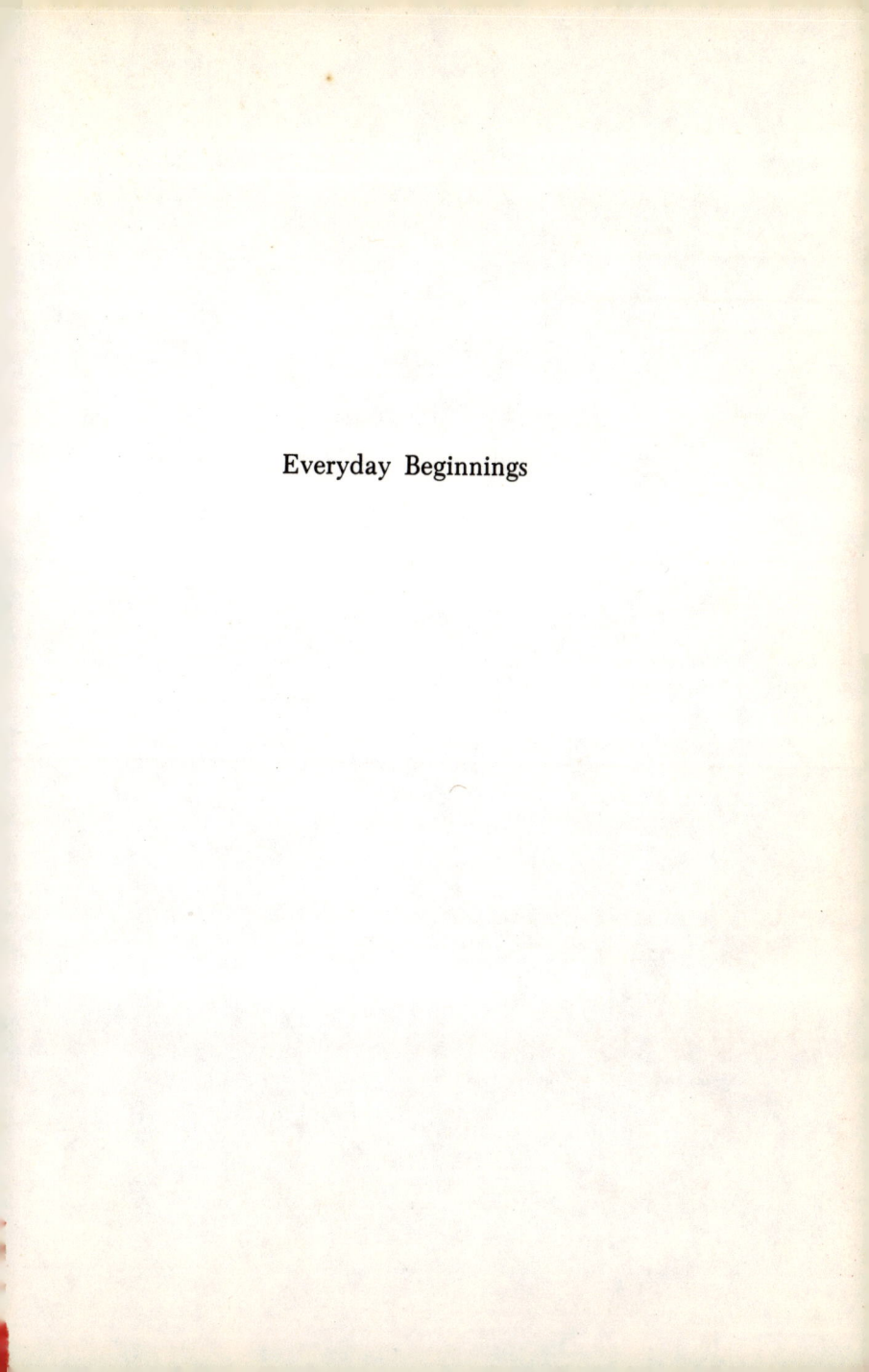

Everyday Beginnings

Everyday Beginnings

Patricia A. Simmons

BROADMAN PRESS
Nashville, Tennessee

© Copyright 1980   Broadman Press

All rights reserved.

4251-77

ISBN 0-8054-5177-3

Verses marked TLB are taken from *The Living Bible.* © Tyndale House Publishers, Wheaton, Illinois, 1971. Used by permission.

Verses marked RSV are from the Revised Standard Version of the Bible, copyrighted 1946, 1952, © 1971, 1973.

Dewey Decimal Classification: 242

Subject headings: WOMEN//MEDITATIONS

Library of Congress Catalog Card Number:80-65387

Printed in the United States of America

Preface

If you have discovered the joy and excitement of knowing that Jesus Christ is really who he said he was, you may also have discovered that becoming a Christian didn't rid you of all your faults and shortcomings. It made you more aware of your imperfections.

I discovered that heart cleaning was something I had to continually work at—like cleaning house. When I began to compare the way I kept house for my Lord and the way I kept house for my family, I found cobwebs in my heart as well as in my house. I discovered a cobweb could be a trap or a bridge. It could be despair or hope—whichever I chose to make it.

God showed me a bridge of hope in a vinegar cruet, a strawberry patch, a dripping faucet, and a bedraggled butterfly.

My thanks to the many friends who gave me encouragement, with special gratitude to those who so generously shared their personal heart cleanings. May all your cobwebs become bridges leading you closer to Jesus Christ.

This book is for all women who have at one time or another discovered cobwebs in their lives, and is dedicated first to God, then to my husband, our children, and my mother and dad.

Contents

God in Me 15

God in Family 41

God in Friends 61

God in Creation 73

Everyday Beginnings

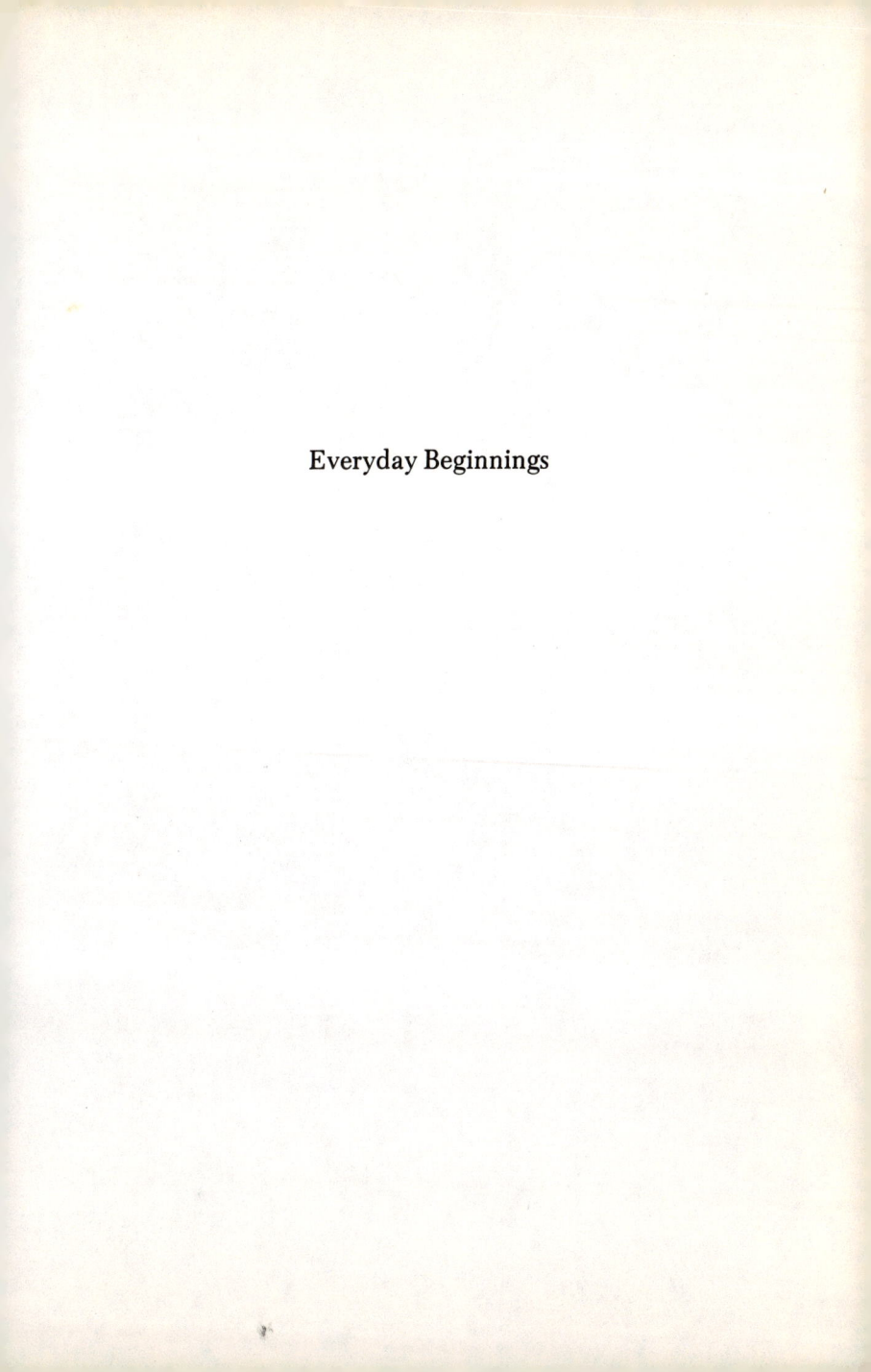

There are two sides to a window
And each must be kept clean.
In order to see from the outside in
The inside, too, must gleam.

Pretend your heart is a window.
Keep it washed and polished from the start.
Your heart looks out on the world
And the world looks in on your heart.

"Create in me a clean heart, O God; and renew a right spirit within me" (Ps. 51:10).

God in Me

Where can you find God?

First somewhere and then everywhere.

He's in the wide open spaces.

He's under the silent stars.

He's on top of a mountain.

Always near—never far.

He's down by the seaside.

He's in a crowded room.

He's with an astronaut

Leaving footprints on the moon.

He's out in the arena;

He's sitting in the grandstand.

First somewhere and then everywhere.

He's within the heart of man.

"I pray that Christ will be more and more at home in your hearts, living within you as you trust in him" (Eph. 3:17, TLB).

The gossamer strands reaching from the fireplace mantel to the ceiling light were revealed by rays of morning sun shining through the kitchen window. A cobweb in my house. The self-pity I was experiencing because of the demands of my family on my time was revealed to me by the light that comes from knowing and following Christ. A cobweb in my heart. Housecleaning and heart cleaning—so different and so alike.

When we bought our present home, the outside was beautiful. A blanket of new snow covered the lawn, and the front windows were sparkling clean. But when we walked through the door the inside was a mass of cobwebs. There was dried food on the cabinet tops, caked chewing gum firmly attached to the floors, and stained carpeting. Even though the interior had been sadly neglected, it did not look hopeless and a good cleaning did wonders! Isn't it great that we don't look hopeless to God and that he can do wonders with a bit of heart cleaning!

"And the Holy Spirit has been at work in your heart, cleansing you with the blood of Jesus Christ and making you to please him" (1 Pet. 1:2, TLB).

During the early years of our marriage we received a cloisonné vase as a gift. I didn't dislike it, but I didn't like it well enough at the time to display it. Later, in redecorating our living room I discovered the perfect place for my vase. While having a decorative arrangement made for it, I learned the value of cloisonné. I took that vase home—carefully—and began thinking about the situation. I was now curious about cloisonné. What made it so valuable? I wanted to know more.

It reminded me of another gift given long ago. "For God so loved the world, that he gave his only begotten Son, that whosoever believeth in him should not perish, but have everlasting life" (John 3:16). For many years I did not know the value of that gift, either. He was there in the background somewhere, stored away like my vase, to be taken out only when I needed him. Then I discovered that instead of being in the background, he was in me, and I began to learn the true meaning of value.

"We have this treasure in earthen vessels" (2 Cor. 4:7).

This morning God asked me if I were a hothouse Christian. I immediately felt like a small child who had just had his hands spanked! A hothouse is an enclosed glasshouse used for growing plants in regulated temperatures and humidity. Do I have to be kept in a glasshouse, sheltered from life, protected from the ups and downs that strengthen and build faith? Flowers can be forced to bloom in such an environment, but Christians whose blooms radiate the beauty of Christ have not been kept in hothouses. They have been exposed to every element of life and through this exposure have become beautiful. Hothouses are used to grow plants and vegetables out of season. God never produces anything out of season—his timing is always perfect.

"When he hath tried me, I shall come forth as gold" (Job 23:10).

A cardinal was singing cheerfully outside my bedroom window, but the predominant sound I heard was a constant drip—drip—drip. In my mind the staccato noise of the leaky faucet was so out of proportion it was more like the banging of a sledgehammer. "Oh God," I prayed, "I want to be able to hear the bird singing instead of the faucet dripping." What I really meant was, "Get rid of that dripping noice." And God listens to the heart! Just at that moment our air conditioner came on, and though the faucet was still dripping I could no longer hear it. I felt a sense of relief until I realized that neither could I hear the song of the bird. Before, though the faucet was dripping, I also had the joy of the bird singing. Now both were gone. What a gentle way to remind me to be careful when I pray. I may get what I ask for at the cost of something more dear.

"For the word of God . . . is a discerner of the thoughts and intents of the heart" (Heb. 4:12).

When I sweep a floor, I don't always move furniture, especially the heavy pieces. I clean around them. Then one day something breaks down and the serviceman comes. He moves out an appliance, and, behold, all the dust and lint, along with an assortment of odds and ends, appear before my eyes. Embarrassed, and with no way to ignore it, I hurry to clean up the mess.

In our hearts God sometimes has to move obstacles that reveal things we would rather not have exposed. When I first began writing for the Lord, things went great. Then came the rejection slips. Nothing was accepted. A special friend asked, "Pat, could pride be the reason?" Well, of course not. Me? Pride! I was half way angry with her for even having the nerve to suggest it. But she had planted the idea, and it would not go away. When I finally accepted it for the truth it was, I realized the validity of the following Scripture verse.

"The pride of thine heart hath deceived thee" (Obad. 1:3).

Ecstatically happy and overflowing with love after accepting Jesus as my Savior, I immediately gave him all of me—I thought! It didn't take long to discover that though I had given him all of me I knew about, as time passed unforeseen parts of me kept popping up that made the giving a continuous process. Some were new to me and a total surprise. Others had been hidden deep inside because I hadn't wanted to think about them. As each is revealed, I give another part of me to God. It's like walking on the beach and finding what the tide has washed in. Sometimes I like what I find and sometimes I don't, but either way I give it to God and start anew again the next day.

"Thou shalt love the Lord thy God with all thy heart, and with all thy soul, and with all thy strength, and with all thy mind" (Luke 10:27).

It was disturbing when God told me I had a yo-yo faith. He gives me a miracle that pulls me up, and then I let circumstances take me down. If you have ever played with a yo-yo, you know how the string with energy exerted through your hand pulls it up and gravity takes it down. It runs smoothly regardless of whether going up or down, as long as the one in control of the string doesn't falter. If my spiritual life is functioning properly with God in control, the down times will not cause me to come unwound and life will flow in a smooth continuing motion. However if I attempt to control the string—or my life—it becomes knotted and unwound.

The children of Israel had a yo-yo faith. When they came to the Red Sea they said, "Wherefore hast thou dealt thus with us?" (Ex. 14:11). God parted the sea. In the wilderness the people murmured against Moses saying, "What shall we drink?" (Ex. 15:24). The bitter water was sweetened. Later hunger came and with it further complaints: "Would to God we had died by the hand of the Lord in the land of Egypt . . . for ye have brought us forth into this wilderness to kill this whole assembly with hunger" (Ex. 16:3). God provided quail and manna. This yo-yo faith continued throughout their journey.

If my faith depends on my circumstances, then it will be a yo-yo faith—because circumstances are not always favorable. It is easy to believe when we see, but true faith is believing when we do not see.

"Faith is the substance of things hoped for, the evidence of things not seen" (Heb. 11:1).

Don had frequently encouraged me to carry a large stick with me on my morning walk, as a weapon to ward off unfriendly dogs. Sometimes I did, but usually I forgot. One morning as I walked, I heard this foghorn bark that sounded as if it were coming from nothing smaller than a Great Dane or a Doberman or a combination of both. I breathed a prayer, "Be not afraid, only believe" (Mark 5:36). I was almost holding my breath when I saw my adversary on the other side of a fenced yard. As I whispered "Thank you, Lord," I could see so clearly how the blood of Jesus Christ provides the fence between me and evil. It was as if he said, "I died on that cross making my blood the fence to protect you. It doesn't matter how much the dogs bark or what is out there, I am the fence around you and you need not be afraid."

My mother once told me that during my early years of marriage she almost dreaded coming to visit me. My obsession with having an immaculate house made her uncomfortable. She was afraid she would track in some dirt. An exceptionally good housekeeper should be complimented, but at that time in my life my priorities were mixed-up.

Remember when Jesus and his disciples stayed with Martha? Luke tells us "They came to a village where a woman named Martha welcomed them into her home. Her sister Mary sat on the floor, listening to Jesus as he talked. But Martha was the jittery type, and was worrying over the big dinner she was preparing. She came to Jesus and said, 'Sir, doesn't it seem unfair to you that my sister just sits here while I do all the work? Tell her to come and help me.' But the Lord said to her, 'Martha, dear friend, you are so upset over all these details! There is really only one thing worth being concerned about. Mary has discovered it—and I won't take it away from her' " (Luke 10:38-42, TLB). Jesus wasn't saying that it was alright for Mary never to work and for Martha to do all the work. He was saying that your first concern should be to get your spiritual life in order and that then you will find more than enough time for all the work that must be done. He was explaining to Martha about priorities.

"For this cause came I unto this hour." These words of Jesus came to me as I walked through a valley of shadows. I realized that I was in this valley facing this situation for this cause—to learn something I could not have understood under any other circumstances.

The circumstance is less important than the way we respond to it. Circumstances sometimes create an atmosphere in which we become trapped in a web not of our own spinning, but for the most part the webs we become entangled in are of our own weaving. Our situation is not necessarily created by God's direction, but it exists by his permission. We look at circumstances instead of what God wants us to see. We continually have two choices. If we are in a difficult situation, we can end up in a self-pity hog-wallow, or we can say, "Thank-you, Lord, for this circumstance in my life. I know you are accomplishing something right now even though I cannot see it at the moment."

"Now is my soul troubled; and what shall I say? Father, save me from this hour: but for this cause came I unto this hour" (John 12:27).

When the Lord revealed to me he wanted me to write for him, I was cautious about sharing such news. Why should anyone believe me? I had never written for publication. Would my telling what God was going to do be a good witness? Sometimes when we feel strongly about something the Lord has revealed to us we are eager to share it, and in doing so may seem boastful without realizing it. I decided that when my first book was released I could share my testimony.

At Capernaum when the tax collectors asked Peter if Jesus paid taxes, he immediately responded "Yes." Then he hastened to Jesus who told him, "Lest we should offend them, go thou to the sea, and cast an hook, and take up the fish that first cometh up; and when thou hast opened his mouth, thou shalt find a piece of money; that take, and give unto them for me and thee" (Matt. 17:27). Peter obeyed instantly. Insofar as we know he didn't tell anyone where he was going and for what purpose, but I have often wondered what he thought about on the way to the sea. There was no need for Peter to tell. This was something between Jesus and him. When Peter had the coin in hand for the taxes, then there was something truly miraculous to share.

"The secret of the Lord is with them that fear him; and he will shew them his covenant" (Ps. 25:14).

Sometimes my walk with our Lord reminds me of an experience with our first cleaning lady. During my second pregnancy I had health difficulties, so Don hired someone to clean our home once a week. She was a delightful person and an excellent worker, but I had never had anyone clean for me before and was concerned she might not do things as I wanted them done. She must have been exasperated with me many times, because I gave all sorts of instructions and advice. One day Don said to me, "Why don't you let her do it her way?" Truthfully, she cleaned house better than I did. She didn't need any instructions from me. I had every reason to trust her completely, just as I have every reason to trust our Lord. But in my walk with him, there have been times when I have even tried to supervise his work! He wants me to have the desires of my heart, but in the way that would be best for me—and my way is not always best. I can be in such a hurry I neglect to spray the dust mop and then about all I do is stir up dust. God creates from dust!

"Rest in the Lord, and wait patiently for him" (Ps. 37:7).

"Commit thy way unto the Lord; trust also in him; and he shall bring it to pass" (Ps. 37:5).

It has been said that tears make rainbows in the soul. Jesus wept at Lazarus's tomb. Some say he wept because he was sharing the sorrow of Mary and Martha. Some believe he wept because he knew Lazarus would prefer not to be brought back to life if given the choice. Recently, when I was "making rainbows" in my soul, I compared myself to a bottle that has not been washed for some time. Layers of dust can collect until it takes a good scrubbing to get it clean. I had been storing up hurt like the layers of dust in that bottle. After so much of it continues to collect—hurt on top of hurt—it takes a good scrubbing to get the soul clean. Maybe tears are God's way of cleansing all this out of my soul. It seemed to me he was using my tears. I was the bottle, and he was shaking the bottle up and down to loosen the dirt. I was tired after the shaking, but in a way that is difficult to explain I felt better. The hurt had not gone away; but the tears, like soothing ointment on a sunburn, had eased the hurt.

"You have seen me tossing and turning through the night. You have collected all my tears and preserved them in your bottle! You have recorded every one in your book" (Ps. 56:8, TLB).

"Today I hit the high spots" or "I skimmed the surface this morning" are phrases familiar to women responsible for cleaning a house. One example of hitting the high spots and cleaning the most obvious is dusting the tabletop and not the table legs. Another is spraying the dust mop and whisking up the surface dust instead of scrubbing the floor. This process gets rid of some dust and rearranges what remains until it settles differently and isn't as noticeable. Have you ever used a feather duster? Feathers dislodge and fall off, until eventually the few remaining feathers barely streak a dusty tabletop. It no longer does a good job hitting the high spots. You notice the feathers gradually falling but don't seem to notice the need for replacement until it is no longer usable.

At times this has happened with my spiritual life. The day I skim the surface with my prayer time and Bible study I am about as usable as that dilapidated feather duster. If I find I am still dwelling on my problems and anxieties after prayer, then I know I am still full of self and not ready to be used of God. I must present myself to God each morning, leaving everything with him so he will have a clean vessel through which to work.

"If anyone purifies himself from what is ignoble, then he will be a vessel for noble use, consecrated and useful to the master of the house, ready for any good work" (2 Tim. 2:21, RSV).

One day a lady who had invited me to speak to her Sunday School class telephoned, asking for a list of my accomplishments to tell about when introducing me. No one had ever asked this of me before, and it resulted in some soul searching on my part. What were my accomplishments? If today were the last day of my life and if God asked me that same question, how would I answer? I immediately began to hope this would not be the last day of my life. How well had I carried my crosses? How many hours had I spent on my knees? Then Jesus gently reminded me that when we pick up our cross to follow him, at that moment it also becomes his cross and the victory is ours! I, myself, have not accomplished anything, but I have accomplished much as I recognize Christ working in and through me.

"I can of mine own self do nothing" (John 5:30), but "I can do all things through Christ which strengtheneth me" (Phil. 4:13).

Today most of us are fortunate enough to have screens over our windows to keep insects out of our homes. Occasionally we need to clean these screens, because dust and other dirt from the outside world collects on them. When this happens we also discover that not as much light gets through and the inside of our house will be less cheery. When we are not in God's will, dust and dirt from the outside world creates a dirty screen between us and God. When we get back in his will, we see things more clearly because we are once again walking in the light of his presence.

"Then spake Jesus again unto them, saying, I am the light of the world: he that followeth me shall not walk in darkness, but shall have the light of life" (John 8:12).

It would be astonishing to know how many things are left permanently undone because they are temporarily put off. One of Satan's most effective tools is getting Christians to put off doing things. The housekeeping chore I am most likely to put off is cleaning the oven. I don't like to clean it. However, if I am having company for dinner and there is the slightest possiblity someone may look inside the oven, I'll clean it before the dinner party because I don't want anyone to see how dirty I can let it get. Now and then my insides remind me of the inside of my oven. On occasion I have thoughts I would want to clean up in a hurry if I knew company could hear them.

One day my mind was full of unkind thoughts when suddenly God turned my thought process around. Was my behavior such that no one would have reason for unkind thoughts about me? There God was, scrubbing at my insides again, as he reminded me "You are so careful to polish the outside of the cup, but the inside is foul with extortion and greed. Blind Pharisees! [Blind me!] First cleanse the inside of the cup, and then the whole cup will be clean" (Matt. 23:26, TLB).

Near our home where I walk is a short, steep hill. At the top I cannot see all the way down, so it is impossible to know what lies at the foot of the hill. Neither can I be sure what is in the road on the way down. However, I can see the road further on, and, because it appears similar to that which I see, I move on, trusting that the part in between will be passable. It has never occurred to me to wonder if there would be a big hole in the road or if a boulder might be across my path. If I would trust God on my spiritual walk as I trust my instincts on such a road as I have just described, my journey would be less difficult. To God mountains of difficulties are as easy to travel as an asphalt road.

"Behold, he cometh leaping upon the mountains, skipping upon the hills" (Song of Sol. 2:8).

Our schools were closed. Streets were considered impassable. Cars were stalled. We were snowbound. What should I do? "Stand thou still a while, that I may show thee the work of God" (1 Sam. 9:27). The snow had forced me to stand still. And I liked it! I was shown the word of God in cleaning a closet. "But thou, when thou prayest, enter into thy closet, and when thou hast shut thy door, pray to thy Father which is in secret; and thy Father which seeth in secret shall reward thee openly" (Matt. 6:6). I was shown the word of God in writing a letter. "Good news from far away is like cold water to the thirsty" (Prov. 25:25, TLB). I was shown the word of God in baking. "Make me thereof a little cake first, and bring it unto me, and after make for thee and for thy son" (1 Kings 17:13). I was shown the word of God in getting reacquainted with my neighbors. "Let every one of us please his neighbor for his good to edification" (Rom. 15:2). Through being forced to stand still, I relearned the joy of hearing and recognizing his "still small voice" (1 Kings 19:12).

Paul's words "You are trying to find favor with God by what you do or don't do on certain days or months or seasons or years" (Gal. 4:10, TLB) brought to my mind the two times a year I used to attend church. I celebrated the birth and resurrection of Jesus—Christmas and Easter. It's suggestive of seasonal housecleaning! Any woman responsible for keeping house will at one time or another decide to really dig in and give the whole place a thorough cleaning. Have you ever had the urge to do spring cleaning after neglecting your house the rest of the year? What a mess! Some household jobs can be seasonal, but too often we postpone what should be done daily and housecleaning becomes a mountainous task. If I serve Christ because of obligation, what I do becomes a task. If I serve him because of dedication, daily activities become opportunities. Hannah Smith in her book *A Christian's Secret of a Happy Life* calls it being a Christian for hire or a Christian for love. When I was a Christian for hire I knew about God. When I became a Christian for love I knew God.

"Serve him with a perfect heart and with a willing mind; for the Lord searcheth all hearts, and understandeth all the imaginations of the thoughts: if thou seek him, he will be found of thee" (1 Chron. 28:9).

One of the most delighful treasures in God's Word has been for me the discovery of how an old familiar Scripture passage can suddenly take on new meaning. This morning when I read "The joy of the Lord is your strength" (Neh. 8:10), I realized my mind had been misinterpreting that message. In prayer I had said, "The joy of the Lord is my strength, but Lord, I don't feel any of that joy today." Now that Scripture verse reads "the joy of the Lord" not "the joy of Pat." When I was a child, the joy of my parents in my achievements was an inspiration that encouraged me to try even harder things. It was part of a strengthening process toward maturity. It is the same with a child of God. When through him I have conquered some temptation, or when I have finally been able to give him my burden and leave it with him, he has joy in this accomplishment. Because of his joy I have gained additional strength for spiritual maturity.

As a bride I was ready and eager to see to it that our home stayed clean. I found that I don't enjoy my home as much when it is cluttered and in a mess as I do when it is neat and clean. As the bride of Christ I have a responsibility to maintain his spiritual house. "Know ye not that ye are the temple of God, and that the Spirit of God dwelleth in you?" (1 Cor. 3:16). He lives in me, yet there are times that were it not for his grace he would probably move out. This was one of those days. I yelled at my husband. I spoke unkind words. I used every frown muscle I possessed. I know what love is, but this day I experienced resentment, self-pity, and almost everything else that love isn't! I am thankful that God still loves me. He doesn't like what I did, but he still loves me—and I have some "picking up" to do.

There is a freeway in the South that has telephones placed at one-half mile intervals with the sign "Travelers' Aid Call Box" above each phone. This is a convenience travelers with car trouble certainly appreciate. When I looked at those boxes I thought how grateful I am it isn't necessary to wait for one-half mile intervals before I can talk to God! I don't even have to get out of my car. I'm also thankful some operator isn't timing my conversation so that at the end of three minutes I either have to stop talking or put money into a meter.

"The Lord is near to all who call upon him" (Ps. 145:18, RSV).

On my way to a "pick your own strawberries patch" I prayed, "Lord, if there is a meditation in the strawberry patch, let me see it." He answered my prayer. An assortment of emotions surfaced when I discovered someone in front of me briskly picking only the large, choice berries from the row assigned to me. First I was surprised, next provoked, and then resentful. I was getting the leftovers. I thought of Ruth and her gratitude as she gathered and gleaned the leftovers after the reapers. My attitude wasn't one of gratitude. I thought of the workers in the vineyards who labored one hour and received the same pay as those who had worked all day. By choosing only large berries, the poacher could fill his basket in fifteen minutes, while it would take me twice that time to fill mine with smaller berries. Yet either would provide a delicious shortcake, and there were plenty of berries for both of us. Then God reminded me of Boaz who owned the field from which Ruth had gleaned. His first thought had been of Ruth, not of what she was taking from him. I had thought of myself and resented what someone was taking from me. "Whatsoever is right, that shall ye receive" (Matt. 20:7*b*).

God permitted someone to infringe on my portion of the strawberry patch for a reason. No wonder I received small berries. My greater need was for spiritual food, but God in his gracious goodness provided both kinds.

God in Family

Things were going wrong that day.
The children were driving her crazy.
Hubby spilled paint on her nice clean floor.
Baby picked the neighbor's prize daisies.

"God, I know I asked for patience," she said,
"But could I take that prayer back?
Because if I have to go through this to get it
I don't believe I'll last!"

Just at that moment there appeared a small lad.
A bouquet of violets was all that he had.
"I picked 'em for you," he said with a smile,
And suddenly everything seemed worthwhile.

"Love is patient and kind" (1 Cor. 13:4, RSV).

When Paul was being taken to Rome as a prisoner it was winter—the most dangerous time of the year to be at sea. Their ship was in a storm of typhoon strength that lasted fourteen days. All cargo was dumped overboard. The counsel was to kill the prisoners so they wouldn't escape. The ship was wrecked. Paul gathered everyone together and said, "Be of good cheer" (Acts 27:22). In my journey of motherhood I relate to Paul on this journey to Rome. Sibling storms seldom last fourteen days, but as they gather toward typhoon strength two days can seem like two weeks! I have considered dumping my cargo; and occasionally my crew probably has considered disposing of me. When I sense a storm gathering with the possibility of a shipwreck in our daily lives, Paul's words "Be of good cheer" serve as encouragement and a reminder that all on board made it to shore. So shall we.

Can you imagine how God must have chuckled when he made it possible for me to thank him for body odor? Some friends telephoned and invited Cathy and me to attend a gospel concert. Their son picked us up, and even with the car windows open, bringing the fresh air in, we had moments of breath holding. When we arrived at church, the young people sat apart from us. I was spared the proximity of the odor, but was sympathetic with Cathy. After the concert was over and we had returned home, she called me to her room. Exuberant with excitement, she said in one breath, "Mother, did you smell body odor? It was so bad I thought I couldn't stand it. Then I decided to ask Jesus to make it smell like strawberries. And you know what, Mother, I smelled strawberries and never noticed the body odor again! Wasn't that neat? And the concert was beautiful." There were no actual boxes of strawberries in that sanctuary, but someone may have been wearing strawberry scent. Whatever, God was there and "with God all things are possible" (Mark 10:27). Because of this experience Cathy walks a bit closer with our Lord, and we thank him for it. Today when something over which we have no control bothers us we are inclined to say "Ask to smell strawberries."

"So faith, hope, love abide, these three; but the greatest of these is love" (1 Cor. 13:13, RSV). Faith, hope, and love are revealed in Jochebed's decision to place her son Moses in the bulrush basket and then gently place it in the edge of the river. She wanted to save his life, so she performed the heartbreaking task of parting with her child. Her faith was steadfast, and Moses' life was spared. Her hope was fulfilled, and he was returned to the God of his infancy. Her love was rewarded, and she received him back again into her arms. Although circumstances may differ, the lesson remains for today: in order to keep our children we must let them go. I am two people now. One of me is looking forward to our son leaving, because there will be less housework and more opportunity for those things I've never before had time to do. But the other me is crying inside because she doesn't want him to go. Like Jochebed, in faith, hope, and love, I will do what is best for him by giving him his opportunity for life.

Whether to yourself or to another, promises made and never kept are worse than no promises. While cleaning house have you ever seen a cobweb and left it, promising yourself you would get it later? It continues to collect lint and dust until you get back to it. Have you ever needed to ask forgiveness, and being fully aware of the need still put it off? The day I called Donald a horrid, degrading name we were all shocked, and I was ashamed and humiliated. I would have spanked our children had I heard them use such a word, and I used it on their father in their presence. "Out of the abundance of the heart his mouth speaks" (Luke 6:45, RSV). I knew I must ask forgiveness from God, Donald, and the children, but it took me three days to do it. That cobweb in my heart, the need to ask and receive forgiveness, kept collecting guilt until I did something about it. I could see no way God could take the word I had spoken and make anything good come from it, but praise him, "with God all things are possible" (Mark 10:27).

My asking forgiveness led into one of the best discussions on Christianity we have ever had. We discussed how being a Christian doesn't make you perfect but does make you more aware of your imperfections. We related to Paul's dilemma: "For I do not do the good I want, but the evil I do not want is what I do" (Rom. 7:19, RSV). Once again I saw how "all things work together for good to them that love God, to them who are the called according to his purpose" (Rom. 8:28). Thanks to a forgiving God and a forgiving family, the shame and humiliation I experienced is now like a healed wound. The scar remains, but it no longer pains.

Today I have been hurting inside because one of our children is hurting. I went out on our patio with a booklet of selected Scripture references recommended to be helpful under given situations. A butterfly, symbolic of hope and the resurrection, lit on the arm of my chair. I watched it open and close its wings, which were misshapen and bedraggled as if it, too, had met with hardship and hurting in its life. Then, lifting in flight, it settled gently on the open booklet in my hand and the scripture passage it was touching read, "And all thy children shall be taught of the Lord; and great shall be the peace of thy children" (Isa. 54:13). I thought of the crucifixion and how at the time it was the darkest day in history. Then I thought of the resurrection three days later. Somehow I knew God was telling me through this butterfly that our child, even with his scars, would be all right and that if I would wait three days I would look at this particular hurt from a different perspective. Returning into the house, I opened the Bible to Mark 16:20 to read about the resurrection, "And they went forth . . . the Lord working with them, and confirming the word with signs following." I thanked God for sending the butterfly as reassurance and confirmation of his word that our child would be all right.

Thoroughly exasperated with our twenty-year-old who was ignoring the guidance we had carefully suggested, I practically threw the cake in the oven. Setting the timer I asked, "What next, God!" Silence. Then I realized that there are some things in life that must run their course. It takes forty-five minutes to bake this cake. It will not bake any sooner. If I turn the oven temperature higher, the cake will burn; if I reduce the heat the texture of the cake will be ruined. I do not stand in front of the oven constantly watching the cake. I prepared it for baking and placed it in the oven, and now I wait.

We prepared this child for life the very best way we could. It is not necessary to watch or know his every move. He has to make his own mistakes and achieve his own goals and learn from both. If we attempt to hurry him up or slow him down, we are doing him an injustice. There is no way to give a twenty-year-old the maturity that comes from the actual experience of forty years of living. He needs all the time allotted him by God to become the individual he is meant to be. "When the fulness of the time was come, God sent forth his Son" (Gal. 4:4). In "the fulness of his time" he will guide our son to maturity.

While one of our children was suffering a deep disappointment, I was sitting on the back steps of our patio looking up into the heavens talking to God. A small white cloud came into view, and how God used that little cloud! It led me out of the wilderness into the light again. "And the Lord went before them by day in a pillar of a cloud, to lead them the way" (Ex. 13:21). He told me this disappointment was nothing more than a little white cloud. The cloud would soon disintegrate and disappear, and life would keep moving on. The disappointment our child was experiencing would in time be forgotten as he moved on in life toward new goals and new horizons. Because he had learned from the experience it could be considered a new beginning rather than an ending. "For what is your life? It is even a vapour, that appeareth for a little time, and then vanisheth away" (Jas. 4:14).

I feel a depth of love in the prayer Jesus said for the disciples that has led me to use his words when I pray for our children. "I pray for them: . . . which thou hast given me; for they are thine." These children were trusted to our care for a few short years, but they are not ours. "I have given them thy word." The Holy Bible. "Sanctify them through thy truth: thy word is truth. I pray not that thou shouldest take them out of the world, but that thou shouldest keep them from the evil." We cannot. "As thou hast sent me into the world, even so have I also sent them into the world." Go with them. "Holy Father, keep through thine own name those whom thou hast given me, that they may be one, as we are." Thank you. (Bible quotations are from John 17.)

There is more to see and learn in one day than it is possible to accomplish. In his great wisdom God tells us to "Live one day at a time" (Matt. 6:34, TLB). His plan for us does not include seeing around corners. I remember when our first baby was placed in my arms. Had the doctor told me at that moment, "He will have an accident the year he gets his driver's license" or "He will break his leg while skiing," I wonder if we would ever have let him drive or ski? Yet he's grown now, and we survived the crises we could not foresee by meeting them as they came, with each experience providing its own unique opportunity for growth. God doesn't want anyone to have a broken leg, but we can thank him for what we learn with a broken leg that would never have been learned otherwise.

We so want to protect our children from hurt that we tend to forget they, too, must taste the bitter in order to savor the sweet. "In every thing give thanks: for this is the will of God in Christ Jesus concerning you" (1 Thess. 5:18).

Today another person caused someone I love to hurt, not physical hurt but the more tender and painful hurt that comes from being unjustly accused and then rejected. I know the accuser would not believe me should I speak the truth, so I shall remain silent. Prompted by the Father, Jesus spoke boldly on occasions and at other crucial times remained silent. A friend of mine, in discussing the beneficial work of speech therapists, gently added this thought: "Perhaps we need some 'silence therapists' also; or better still, we need to recognize the presence and power of the Holy Spirit along this line." In Isaiah 53:7 we have the prophecy, "He was oppressed, and he was afflicted, yet he opened not his mouth." Words spoken in haste under stress are often regretted, but there are few times we ever regret remaining silent. "The Lord shall fight for you, and ye shall hold your peace" (Ex. 14:14).

A lad of eleven years was sitting crosslegged on the grass beside the Scotch pine that had been his first Christmas tree. I knew he would be in the house soon to talk. It was easy to tell when something was on his mind. As the back door slammed, he said, "Mom, you really believe in that prayer bit, don't you?" I knew he was thinking of the ball game he was scheduled to pitch that evening in the finals of the summer league. God provides such beautiful opportunities for sharing with our children. The poem below shares the content of our conversation that afternoon.

> "Mom," he said, "Will it help to pray?
> I'd sure like to win that game today."
>
> She looked thoughtfully at her young son.
> His question was an important one.
>
> "God loves one team as much as the other,"
> Came the soft reply from the loving mother.
>
> "It always helps to pray, my son,
> If the prayer is not a selfish one.
>
> "Tell him that you'd like to win,
> But should you lose, don't question him."

"Trust in the Lord with all thine heart; and lean not unto thine own understanding" (Prov. 3:5).

In the children's story "Rumpelstiltskin," a young girl's father, trying to gain the attention of the king, bragged that his daughter could spin straw into gold. Anxious because she was not making her customary A in a class, Cathy expressed her frustration by saying, "Mother, I hope you and Daddy don't expect me to spin gold." Occasionally parents are guilty of this, but our heavenly King never asks or expects more than we are capable of giving. Over and over again we discover that with Christ working through us we can do more than we realize.

The lame man at the Temple gate was hoping to receive alms when Peter spoke to him, " 'Silver and gold have I none; but such as I have give I thee: In the name of Jesus Christ of Nazareth rise up and walk.' And he took him by the right hand, and lifted him up: and immediately his feet and ankle bones received strength. And he leaping up stood, and walked, and entered with them into the temple, walking, and leaping, and praising God" (Acts 3:6-8). When Peter gave the command, the lame man could have said, "But I can't! You know I'm lame!" Instead he was obedient; he tried. First he received strength, next he stood, then he walked, and, most important of all, he praised God. God provided the ability for more than he had ever dreamed possible. Sometimes it takes a great deal of courage to "rise up and walk."

Our son, working as a relief pitcher, was sent into a game with the bases already loaded. He had a full count on the batter, who proceeded to foul off the next eight pitches before grounding out. Afterwards Brad said, "I figured I'd get him eventually!" Another attitude could have been, "If he keeps this up, he'll hit one for sure!" A positive attitude versus a negative attitude. Trust versus doubt.

Had I been on the mission as one of the twelve spies sent to survey Canaan I wonder if I would have been one of the ten who came back and said, "We be not able to go up against the people; for they are stronger than we." Or would I have been like Joshua and Caleb who said, "Let us go up at once, and possess it; for we are well able to overcome it" (Num. 13:30-31)? Ten were negative and filled with fear, even though they had seen the tremendous potential for settling there. Two were positive, even though there was something to overcome.

When circumstances look like giants, I am looking at the circumstances instead of Jesus. When I get my eyes back on Jesus, the giant immediately shrinks in size. If we trust God, we will face our giants with a positive attitude, and like Caleb and Joshua will find ourselves "well able to overcome it."

My flowers and plants have often been flattened by the force of the water coming from the spray nozzle of our garden hose. However, the water given to those plants was life-giving, and as time passed it nourished their roots. The plants, drawn once again toward the sun, became more beautiful than before. As I watched our daughter leaving the tennis court after a humbling, shut-out defeat, she reminded me of a flower flattened by the water. The defeat or drenching she received on the tennis court would strengthen her roots. She would learn and grow from it, and once again be drawn toward the Son, becoming more beautiful than before because of the experience.

"Showers soften the earth, melting the clods and causing seeds to sprout across the land" (Ps. 65:10, TLB).

When our son went away for a summer job he left his sports car at home. One day while it was in our garage his dad accidentally put a tiny scratch on the hood. We were not particularly concerned. If you didn't know where the scratch was, you could hardly find it. By the time my son returned we had forgotten it. Three months later he gave his sister permission to drive the car while he was gone on a short vacation. Upon his return he discovered the scratch, and I learned later that he questioned her about it. She agreed to wash, wax, and polish the car to buff out the scratch. She knew how it happened, but didn't tell her brother. When I suggested telling him about it, she replied, "Oh, let's not, Mother. I don't mind taking the blame for it, and this way Dad won't be bothered with it." I am not sure I could have done what she did. Today she taught me a little more about the way of love. Love "does not hold grudges and will hardly even notice when others do it wrong" (1 Cor. 13:5, TLB).

The day we watched some robins teaching their offspring to fly, I observed patience in action. It was as if the parents had drawn a large circle and the baby birds were not allowed beyond it. If one ventured past the boundary, the wing of a parent would gently guide it back into the circle. If one appeared to be having difficulty reaching the safety of a branch, the parents didn't show frustration or anxiety. They remained nearby in the tree giving an occasional chirp of encouragement while the little one learned to fly on its own, yet in an unexplainable way revealing their faith and confidence in the ability of the struggling little one to achieve its place in the bird kingdom.

The robin parents could not fly for their little ones. We cannot live our children's lives for them. Like those robins, when we have done what we can as parents we must trust God to help our children find their place in his world, standing on his promise: "The Lord will perfect that which concerneth me" (Ps. 138:8).

"For He will give his angels charge of you to guard you in all your ways" (Ps. 91:11, RSV). Guardian angels—available to us! I have claimed this guarding not only for my own children but also for those who will someday be their marriage partners lest others might forget.

> My prayer today is for one
> Whom I have never met.
> Care for her and guide her,
> Lest others might forget.
>
> She'll be a bride someday;
> The groom will be our son.
> Grant her wisdom, God
> And compassion for everyone.
>
> Give her a sense of humor
> To help her enjoy life.
> Give her strength and courage
> When she faces strife.
>
> Teach her to have hope;
> Let her faith be strong.
> Surround her with thy love
> And keep her for our son.

I pray today for a small lad
Whom I have never met.
Guide him in his growing years,
Lest others might forget.

Let him be stalwart, strong, and brave,
But let him be humble, too.
Give him hope and a faith that's deep
And wisdom that comes from you.

Help him find his place in life;
Guide him as he makes that choice.
Let it be an occupation
In which he'll always rejoice.

As the days of his life pass by
Be ever present at his side.
For when this boy becomes a man
Our daughter will be his bride.

God in Friends

A friend is to love.
It's someone to care
Someone to listen
And someone to share.

It's someone who knows
When you are down
Then helps pull you up
By just being around.

"A friend loves at all times" (Prov. 17:17, RSV).

"Then Simon Peter having a sword drew it, and smote the high priest's servant, and cut off his right ear" (John 18:10). Listening to a friend vent her frustration and anger at an injustice done to her, I gently inquired, "Have you tried to see this through the eyes of Jesus?" She snapped, "No, I'm Peter and I'm chopping off ears." We both were momentarily stunned by her reply, then simultaneously burst into laughter. Jesus used a delightful way to get his message across. We recalled Peter's action in Gethsemane and our tendency to be like him instead of like Jesus. Jesus told Peter, "Put up thy sword into the sheath: the cup which my father hath given me, shall I not drink it?" (John 18:11). Then Jesus healed the servant who lost his ear as a result of Peter's temper.

Calm your anger. This circumstance in your life is there because you have something to learn from it. Quit fighting. Stand still and drink the water offered you. Your thirst will be quenched, and your hurt will be healed.

As we sat in church this morning, I watched Suzanne, the small, adopted daughter of one of our church families. She stepped in front of her mother and with hands outstretched toward her father attempted to climb into his lap. He smiled and gently lifted her to him. She immediately put her head on his shoulder, where she rested quietly throughout the remainder of the service. How often I struggle and strain, attempting or striving for something through self-effort when if I would turn to God with outstretched hands he would lift me up. The confidence and trust Suzanne displayed toward her adopted father is what God wants for me, his adopted child.

"Ye have received the Spirit of adoption, whereby we cry, 'Abba,' Father. The Spirit itself beareth witness with our spirit, that we are the children of God" (Rom. 8:15-16).

A few days after our son was injured in an automobile accident in which his life was miraculously spared, I was still in the process of realizing my insides somewhat resembled a bowl of gelatin not quite set—kind of shaky! I was quoting Scripture passages aloud in an almost frantic manner—a bit like fighting off an army single-handed. In a telephone conversation with a friend I explained what I was doing. She gently suggested: "Pat, there are times to use the Bible as a sword and times to use it as a pillow. You are using it as a sword and swinging it in circles. Try using it as a pillow and lay your head down and rest on it." The churning and turning of my insides began to respond as if to a soothing sedative. I was reminded of when Sennacherib was preparing to invade Judah and King Hezekiah calmed his people by telling them, "With us is the Lord our God to help us, and to fight our battles. And the people rested themselves upon the words of Hezekiah, king of Judah" (2 Chron. 32:8). I rested myself upon the words of my friend and learned the true significance of speaking "a word in season to him that is weary" (Isa. 50:4).

Once when I was absorbing, and envying a little, the wisdom and knowledge and serenity of my dear Christian friend who was eighty-seven years young, I began to think about the instant products in our supermarkets. Today we can buy instant mashed potatoes, instant pudding, instant cereal, or just about instant anything. Most of us have at sometime wished for instant patience, instant knowledge, or instant maturity.

Some prayer requests are granted instantly, but God sometimes asks us to wait in order to receive his fullest blessing. This is like a package of instant food versus a recipe prepared from "scratch," with each ingredient added at the proper moment. Understanding and appreciation come through completing a recipe one step at a time. Occasionally I think it would be easier to be an instantly mature Christian. But as I listen to those whose faith has been made from "scratch," I find they have much to share. Then I am glad God does have a recipe for my life and that he knows when it is time to stir in a bit of waiting, a dash of forgiveness, a cup of tears, and all those ingredients that go toward making me into the person he wants me to be.

"For because of our faith, he has brought us into this place of highest privilege where we now stand, and we confidently and joyfully look forward to actually becoming all that God has had in mind for us to be" (Rom. 5:2, TLB).

After seeing me out walking at 6:00 AM for the third straight morning, Johnny, our service station attendant, perplexed but smiling, said, "Where are you going?" I replied, "I walk two and one-half miles every morning. Aren't you proud of me?" As I continued my walk and thought about what I had just said, I asked myself, "Why did you add, 'Aren't you proud of me?' " Why should it be important to me to have people proud of me? It isn't necessary for me to prove anything to my husband, my children, or anyone. Those people who know me either see what I hope is there or they see through me if it isn't! Then I began to think of the ways I could have answered Johnny. Had I replied, "Watching the world wake up!" he, too, might have awakened to some special part of God's creation.

"Let no corrupt communication proceed out of your mouth, but that which is good to the use of edifying" (Eph. 4:29).

"And walk in love, as Christ also hath loved us, and hath given himself for us an offering and a sacrifice to God for a sweet-smelling savour" (Eph. 5:2). The pain mirrored in the eyes of my friend revealed anguish. Its depth was known only to God and to her. Still she smiled. Her smile must have been "a sweet savour unto the Lord." God described to Moses, "A burnt sacrifice, an offering made by fire, of a sweet savour unto the Lord" (Lev. 1:13). The psalmist David said, "The sacrifices of God are a broken spirit: a broken and a contrite heart, O God, thou wilt not despise" (Ps. 51:17). My friend had all of these, and in the midst of a fiery furnace, smiling through her tears, her love for Jesus still shone through. Her friends were drawing from her strength. Somehow I know Jesus was feeling her hurt. At the same time I'm sure he was smiling with her because he knew the dross was being consumed and gold was being refined. Paul said it was our "reasonable service" to "present" our "bodies a living sacrifice, holy, acceptable unto God" (Rom. 12:1). My friend was serving.

When Brad was a small boy and first discovered his shadow, he would race after it, laughing and trying to jump on it. He would hide around corners, then leap out and try to catch it. He discovered his shadow was a part of him; and yet he also discovered the necessity of standing in a certain place in order for light to reveal his shadow. To a child this is a simple, delightful discovery, but as time passes, the word *shadow* takes on new and different meanings. On a humid, hot day the shadow of a tree provides a shade where we can find rest from the heat. I have a friend who refers to God's shadow as her umbrella. When circumstances seem overwhelming, she says she is out from under her umbrella—away from God and standing in the heat. She needs the comforting, cooling shade of his presence. Because Jesus is in us he is a part of us like our shadow, and we must stand in the light of his presence in order to rest in his shadow.

"He that dwelleth in the secret place of the most High shall abide under the shadow of the Almighty" (Ps. 91:1).

One afternoon about two weeks following the death of a friend, we invited her husband and his visiting granddaughter to our home for dinner. While I was preparing the meal my thoughts were on the warm, beautiful friendship we had shared with Tommy and Sunbeam, beginning when Don and I were teenagers and continuing through the years. They had become like a third set of grandparents to our children, and we loved them dearly. I found myself wishing that she could see her husband was all right and was enjoying his granddaughter's visit. I wished she could know that he was still visiting in our home. I made a score of other wishes, when it occurred to me that it wasn't necessary or important for her to see this. What was important was that we continue to express our love for them both by showing our love for Tommy.

One morning as I was preparing to go to the hospital to sit with an invalid, I was feeling guilty inside because of mixed emotions about going. You see I wanted to go and I didn't want to go. God brought to my mind the words of Jesus, "Father, if thou be willing, remove this cup from me: nevertheless not my will, but thine, be done" (Luke 22:42). Suddenly I knew it was not wrong to feel this way so long as I went on and did what needed to be done. Along with this thought came a joyous feeling of release because my guilt was gone. Then I found I was eagerly looking forward to going to the hospital. Sometimes we have to do certain things when we would rather do something else. God's leading isn't always down the path we like best.

She dashed into my kitchen, her face alive with joy! "Pat! Guess what God told me through Grandma's vinegar cruet?" Waking up at four o'clock in the morning out of a sound sleep, my friend said she had sat straight up in bed wondering why in the world she was thinking about her grandmother's vinegar cruet. Her grandmother had given her this cut glass vinegar cruet, a treasured family possession. The grandmother frequently called with suggestions of how to wash it, when to use it, and where to put it. "Then I knew what the Lord was telling me," she smiled. "Though Grandma had given me the vinegar cruet, she was still clinging to it." God revealed to my friend that even though she thought she had given her burden to him, she was much like Grandma in that she kept advising him of ways he could handle her situation. She kept possession by trying to direct the Lord. "Woe to the man who fights with his Creator. Does the pot argue with its maker? Does the clay dispute with him who forms it, saying, 'Stop, you're doing it wrong!' or the pot exclaim, 'How clumsy can you be!'?" (Isa. 45:9, TLB). Rejoicing in the freedom from her burden and out of his way, my friend knew he would get on with what needed to be done.

God in Creation

Glittering stars
A moonlight sky
Baby robins
Learning to fly

Four seasons
Changing weather
Earth and oceans
Ice and heather

Races of people
Rainbows, too
Blending together
Different hues

God's creation
Nothing compares
Given with love
Meant to share.

"And God saw every thing that he had made, and, behold, it was very good" (Gen. 1:31).

This morning I saw a bird perched on a telephone wire with his head lifted toward the heavens, singing with obvious enthusiasm and joy. It sounded as if he were singing "Rejoice! Rejoice! Rejoice!" I thought that in a prettier picture he would have been placed on a leafy branch of a lovely tree. The lesson for me here was twofold. Like Paul, if I could learn "in whatsoever state I am, therewith to be content" (Phil. 4:11), then I too should be able to shout "Rejoice! Rejoice! Rejoice!" and truly mean it as that bird did. The joy of the bird on the ugly barren wire added beauty to otherwise desolate surroundings. Had he been singing in a beautiful setting it would have been the same song, but I might not have noticed him so readily.

"Rejoice in the Lord alway: and again I saw, Rejoice" (Phil. 4:4).

Our newly moved lawn looked pretty, even with the dandelions springing up again. Dandelions, I thought, like people, are not either all good or all bad. They are edible, children pick them for bouquets, and when they go to seed it is great fun to pluck them and blow the seeds in all directions. If we could bounce back as quickly from our disappointments as the dandelion bounces back when it is trampled upon and be equally as perky, we would truly be a witness to our faith in Christ. The deep, deep roots of the dandelion make it the sturdy, resilient plant it is.

"As ye have therefore received Christ Jesus the Lord, so walk ye in him: Rooted and built up in him, and stablished in the faith, as ye have been taught, abounding therein with thanksgiving" (Col. 2:6-7).

Shortly after I accepted Christ as my Savior I began to regret not having known him sooner and brood about all the wasted years that could have been lived for him. How precious and tender was his message! He brought to my thoughts all the varieties of flowers and the way they bloom at different seasons during the year, each with its own special loveliness. The crocus and jonquil are the announcers of spring, while the geranium in its splendor says summer has arrived. We have the chrysanthemum that introduces autumn, and the poinsettia that brings its beauty to the heart of winter. It is good that people can come to know Christ at any season of life. If it were only possible to become a Christian when a teenager, many of us would never bloom! When a person in his golden years discovers Christ it is like finding springtime in winter. Acceptance of Christ into your heart, whenever it may be, is what makes that season special. Others who may not know him and who are in the same season of life see a change—see a new bloom—and receive renewed hope where there may have been despair.

"I am still not all I should be but I am bringing all my energies to bear on this one thing: Forgetting the past and looking forward to what lies ahead" (Phil. 3:13, TLB).

"He sendeth the springs into the valleys" (Ps. 104:10). Having grown up on a farm in the Midwest without plumbing in our home, I learned to appreciate the cold, refreshing, clear water of a spring. Spring water is moving water—alive! When a spring comes out of the earth, dirt, rocks, and obstacles are pushed aside as the fresh water finds its way to the surface. Now and then it becomes necessary for God to show us the springs in our valleys. We scramble around the hillside searching, so intent on our thirst that we miss the location of the spring. God permits certain obstacles to be removed from within us in order that his "living water" may come to the surface. It hurts at the time, but when the removal is complete we become like that spring—moving, fresh, alive, and useful.

"But whosoever drinketh of the water I shall give him shall never thirst; but the water that I shall give him shall be in him a well of water springing up into everlasting life" (John 4:14).

We have a beautiful flowering tree in our yard. One day we noticed that the bark was buckling and the leaves were falling too soon. The tree was no longer looking healthy. We sought help, and at a great price, provided everything the tree needed for its restoration. We cared, and because we cared we did all we could to restore it and renew the life-giving force within it. Maybe God looks on us as his flowering trees. He cares. He certainly paid a great price for us. He provides everything we need and tells us how it can be ours.

"Seek ye the kingdom of God; and all these things shall be added unto you" (Luke 12:31).

Early this morning our world was refreshed with a spring shower. The air smelled so pure, and everything looked fresh and clean. A short distance up the street I saw a speck of red against a tall evergreen. Slowing my pace as I neared the tree, I watched in anticipation of the bird flying away. It didn't move, and when I was even with it I discovered my cardinal was in reality a small red rose. Looking closer, I could see leaves attached to a branch, and near the ground was another rose. That evergreen and that rosebush, totally different yet intertwined, could be compared to our outward appearance and our innermost self. How many times have I looked only at the outside of someone and missed finding the roses hidden in them by my failure to look to the inside.

"That which I see not teach thou me" (Job 34:32).

This morning I saw a cloud formation shaped like a dragon. Recalling how I had shared this imaginative cloud game as a pastime with our children, I chuckled aloud, thinking I would have won first prize this time. Glancing again toward the sky, I discovered my dragon beginning to disintegrate. I'm exceptional at creating dragons that don't exist, so I would have fit right in with the women on their way to the tomb on resurrection morning. Their concern about how to roll the stone away from the tomb had become a dragon in their minds, yet when they arrived the stone was already rolled away. Their dragon had disintegrated before they arrived. They had done all their fretting for nothing. How often we try to move into the future by being concerned over something that may never come to pass. Jesus said, "Don't be anxious about tomorrow. God will take care of your tomorrow too" (Matt. 6:34). Don't be rolling stones away before you get there!

The power of my God and Creator is overwhelmingly real to me when I look at the ocean. Recently while I was gazing in awe upon its magnificence I began to think of the petition so often prayed, "Fill my cup, Lord." God's supply of blessings and power available for us could resemble that ocean. I ask "Fill my cup" when he has an ocean available. Can you imagine anyone missing a cup of water taken from the ocean? God has so much he wants to give, but lack of faith prevents our receiving what is available. Jesus said, "As thou hast believed, so be it done unto thee" (Matt. 8:13). If I ask for a cupful and have only a teaspoonful of faith, my cup will not be overflowing. "Whatever you ask in prayer, believe that you receive it, and you will" (Mark 11:24, RSV).

"He led them through the depths, as through the wilderness" (Ps. 106:9). In Bible lands a wilderness was barren, uncultivated, and usually uninhabited, with some stones here and there but no food available. Such a wilderness would be a confusing place, with nothing to guide you except the sun by day and the stars by night. In the wildernesses of life, lonely and confused, we cry out in despair, seeking guidance from his Son who sees us through.

The darkest, most intense part of night is often referred to as the depth of night. There can be loneliness there, too. Depth is also defined as distance downward, which could mean looking at the world instead of upward to Christ. Distance inward could relate to self. We get so involved with self we almost drown in self-pity, by trying to do things ourselves instead of letting the Lord work through us. Then we have distance backward. We take our eyes off Jesus and look behind us, as the Israelites did when they got tired of the daily manna and wanted the leeks and garlic, or the flavor of the world again.

When I was a girl, I lowered a long, slim, round bucket on a pulley into a deep well to draw water. The depth of the well was determined by where the bucket touched the pure, clear, flowing water. It took a long time for me to pull the bucket of water to the top, just as it sometimes takes a long time to get out of the depths of despair in life. As we drink from the living water that our Lord and Savior provides, we find the nourishment that strengthens. He stretches forth his hand and leads us "through the depths, as through the wilderness."

Watching a robin walking across our street, I knew it could fly quickly away should the need arise. Seeing two squirrels scamper up a tree for safety as they heard my footsteps, I began to consider how God supplies his creatures with the qualities necessary to protect themselves from their predators. Even so each must constantly be alert to the possibility of danger. God also makes available to us everything we need to protect us from sin and evil—the predators of man. "Put on the whole armour of God," said Paul, "that ye may be able to stand against the wiles of the devil." A friend of mine says you can have on the helmet of salvation, but if you leave off the shield of faith you may get punched in the stomach. When I feel like I've had the wind knocked out of me or I've been hurt, I check my list of armor to see if I'm fully covered.

"Stand therefore, having your loins girt about with truth, and having on the breastplate of righteousness; And your feet shod with the preparation of the gospel of peace; Above all, taking the shield of faith . . . And take the helmet of salvation, and the sword of the Spirit, which is the word of God" (Eph. 6:11,14-17).

This morning I saw a rabbit lying dead in the road. It had been hit by a car. I wondered if a dog had been chasing it and the rabbit, so totally absorbed in its fear of the dog, had run directly into the path of a car and lost its life. How often we let some fear totally absorb us until we walk into something much worse than our original fear. "God has not given us the spirit of fear; but of power, and of love, and of a sound mind" (2 Tim. 1:7). Fear does not come from God. Our minds will run away in every direction unless we work at "casting down imaginations . . . and bringing into captivity every thought to the obedience of Christ" (2 Cor. 10:5).

The intermingled shades of orange, yellow, and red moving across the sun presented a panorama of light. One of God's first spoken words was "Let there be light" (Gen. 1:3). Was this the way light appeared on that creation morning? No wonder God created man. The magnificence of a sunrise was something to be shared! This ball of fire called the sun is a life source provided by God as light for the earth. Jesus Christ, the Son of God, is a life source provided by God for the salvation of man. "In him was life; and the life was the light of men" (John 1:4). The beauty of wild flowers and the ugliness of litter along the roadside revealed by the morning sunlight are reminders that the light of Christ reveals both the good and the bad within me. The sun is a cleansing agent. "The blood of Jesus Christ his Son cleanseth us from all sin" (1 John 1:7). The sun has often been used as a compass or guide. We have an infallible guide in the word of God. "Thy word is a lamp unto my feet, and a light unto my path" (Ps. 119:105). If we walk in the sunlight, warmth is there. "If we walk in the light, as he is in the light, we have fellowship one with another" (1 John 1:7), and the warmth of his love is there. He is risen! God's message delivered through a sunrise. "Arise, shine; for thy light is come, and the glory of the Lord is risen upon thee" (Isa. 60:1).

One spring following an unusually severe Ozarks winter, I noticed a tree in our neighborhood that appeared to be dead. I felt a pang of regret when I thought about this loss. All the other trees had been leafed out for a good six weeks. Then a few days later, to my surprise and delight, I discovered tiny green shoots appearing on the dead tree! It was a late bloomer. Had it blossomed when the others did I probably would have admired it as one of many but might have failed to see its individuality. But because it bloomed later its beauty was almost breathtaking. God reminded me through this mimosa tree that some of his children are also late bloomers. He knows the proper timing for all of his creation to come to maturity, whether it be a mimosa tree or one of his children.

"Neither shall your vine cast her fruit before the time in the field, saith the Lord of hosts" (Mal. 3:11).

Hearing some birds shrieking in alarm, I hurried to our backyard to determine the cause. A baby bird had fallen from its nest, and our dog, though nearby and not touching it in any way, was watching with fascination as the baby bird flopped around, not yet old enough to fly. The parent birds were voicing their agitation at the dog's presence. Placing the little one back in the nest, I thought of how our children occasionally leave the security of home before they are prepared and have to be returned to the nest to grow a little stronger before venturing forth again. And then there have been times when I have found myself seemingly "flopping around on the ground," wondering why I am not getting anywhere, and discovering I had launched out on my own strength before I was secure in the strength of the Lord. Maybe I had not read the Word that day or maybe I had neglected my prayer time. Whatever it was, I learned that "They that wait upon the Lord shall renew their strength; they shall mount up with wings as eagles; they shall run and not be weary; and they shall walk, and not faint" (Isa. 40:31).

We have a beautiful weeping willow tree in our backyard, but in order for the tree to retain its beauty it must be pruned occasionally. This morning I noticed some dead branches scattered throughout the tree and realized it was pruning time again. How like what God does in the lives of his children. The sin in my life is like those dead branches and has to be pruned out in order that I might be perfected. Jesus knows when the time is right for pruning. He said, "I am the true vine, and my Father is the husbandman. Every branch in me that beareth not fruit he taketh away: and every branch that beareth fruit, he purgeth it, that it may bring forth more fruit" (John 15:1-2).

This morning I heard a bird singing as if it were so full of joy that the joy was bursting out in song. The bird was completely oblivious to the starlings screeching and carrying on simultaneously in an obvious sound of disgruntled complaining. Out of all that chaotic noise the sound that stood out so much I heard it first was the joyful melody of the bird. One Christian in today's world, living his life daily as Christ would have him do, will be as obvious as the song of that bird, regardless of what else is going on. You don't have to outshout others or forcefully share your faith. The way you live speaks louder than anything you say.

"And, lo, thou art unto them as a very lovely song of one that hath a pleasant voice, and can play well on an instrument: for they hear thy words, but they do them not" (Ezek. 33:32).

The tree outside my kitchen window was exposed in all its winter nakedness. The heavier branches extended outward from the trunk, each laden with smaller branches down to the tiniest twig. It is barren now, but life is there. When spring comes, the tiniest twig holds the bud from which the fruit is created. We have our times of winter nakedness—our times of being purged or prepared for greater usefulness. It is only as we remain attached to our life-giving Vine that we can know with complete confidence that spring will come and there will be fruit again.

"As the branch cannot bear fruit of itself, except it abide in the vine; no more can ye, except ye abide in me" (John 15:4).

The year our son gave me a pin oak tree for Mother's Day, I discovered that this tree does not lose its leaves in the autumn as other trees do. The pin oak leaves, although they turn brown, do not fall off until pushed away by new spring growth. Even though I knew this to be true, I still watched those leaves closely that first winter—not challenging them to fall, but keeping my eyes on them just in case. I thought how this was like a person who is hungering in his soul, hoping that what he hears about Christ is true, and therefore he watches a Christian to see if Christianity is all we say it is.

"Try instead to live in such a way that you will never make your brother stumble by letting him see you doing something he thinks is wrong" (Rom. 14:13, TLB).

The carefree whistle of a boy
A sympathetic smile
The silent presence of a friend
The handclasp of a child.

Morning sunshine at a window
The lilting song of a bird
God has many messengers
Through whom to send his word.

A young girl giving the opening thought for her church youth meeting had been awakened by a mockingbird singing and had taped the melody for the others to hear. But she was unable to tape the joy and love that shone in her eyes as she told how she had related to God through his messenger of song. No mountain was moved, no sea divided, no earthquake, wind, or fire—but there was just as much a miracle because it brought her a special moment with God. Pray God we do not miss the everyday miracle messages in our lives.

"Incline your ear, and come unto me: hear, and your soul shall live" (Isa. 55:3).

Seeing a single deep purple iris in full bloom on the sloping side of a drainage ditch, I thought of the song "Brighten the Corner Where You Are." If the iris hadn't been in bloom it would have gone unnoticed in the midst of many weeds and debris. That iris had not been purposely planted there by anyone. It had washed to its present location, taken root, and bloomed where it was. Often in impatience, we rebel against the circumstances in which we find ourselves, when if we would just take root and accept our situation we could bloom and bring joy to those around us.

"For when your patience is finally in full bloom, then you will be ready for anything, strong in character, full and complete" (Jas. 1:4, TLB).

Ocean waves come in assorted sizes and are usually unpredictable. Surfers know the joy and feeling of exhilaration that come from catching a wave at its crest and riding it in triumph to shore. This summer as I waded into the surf, I stopped with my feet placed slightly apart, bracing myself, and watched the waves crest and break. Sometimes a wave that looked as if it would knock me off my feet would break gently, with practically no force or pressure hitting me at all. Another one appearing to be gentle would break with such force it would nearly bury me in the sand. How often circumstances we face in life resemble those waves. Some incident that appears to be insurmountable is mastered and ridden to shore with little or no difficulty, and that situation we thought we would breeze through trips us up.

Again we are made aware of our need for God as we recognize that "Mightier than the thunders of many waters,/ mightier than the waves of the sea,/the Lord on high is mighty!" (Ps. 93:4, RSV).

The roses on the north side of our house do not bloom as early as those on the south side, even though they are identical. Those that receive more sunshine and light and are better protected from the elements bloom first. People are like this. Those who are exposed to the light of the love of Christ usually bloom sooner than those who are living in the darkness of sin and evil. Which side of the house are you planted on today? Maybe you need to be transplanted.

"Those that be planted in the house of the Lord shall flourish in the courts of our God" (Ps. 92:13).